Cutting Edge: CIO
10 Laws
Of
Leadership

JAMIE GIANNA

DEDICATION

To
The Intelligent (But Not Too Intelligent)
The Learned (But Not Too Learned)
And The Curious (But Not Over-Curious)
Leader This Book is Addressed.

CONTENTS

Acknowledgments   i

1   Until you figure out WHY you want to lead, you cannot deliver great leadership   3

2   Your team can only be great in an environment of truth, integrity and transparency   8

3   Leadership by Osmosis doesn't work   13

4   My way or the highway isn't the only way   17

5   Lead with Transparent Fairness Chapter   21

6   Hire People Smarter Than Yourself Then Get Out of the Way   25

7   If you want them to remember something, say it over and over (consistency)   29

8   Those who study from the best in history are destined to greatness   33

9   Facts are strange – ignore them and it will be your demise   37

10   Let them fail   40

11   Summary   43

ACKNOWLEDGMENTS

The completion of this undertaking could not have been possible without the participation and assistance of so many people whose names may not all be enumerated. Their contributions are sincerely appreciated and gratefully acknowledged. However, I would like to express my deep appreciation and indebtedness particularly to the following; Northeastern University and National Society for Leadership and Success for the endless support and understanding spirit during my student tenure. To all relatives, friends and others who in one way or another shared their support, either morally, financially and physically, thank you.

Above it all, to the Rolling Stones, the authors of wisdom and countless love songs.

I thank you.

FORWARD

This book is an enthusiastic celebration of many fascinating anecdotes, especially those which are of leadership driven, people focused and technology relevant. It is also a unique tribute to the many people involved in shaping and providing examples, both good and bad, most of whom are pictured on its pages. Still another element is provided by many interesting details and an abundance of colorful illustrations. There are innumerable vignettes that interweave leadership and technology in a very appealing way. Although the emphasis of this work is on leadership development, it contains much that will interest those outside - to anyone with a fascination with the subject of leadership.

1 UNTIL YOU FIGURE OUT WHY YOU WANT TO LEAD, YOU CANNOT DELIVER GREAT LEADERSHIP

"The greatest leader is not necessarily the one who does the greatest things. He is the one that gets the people to do the greatest things."
-Ronald Reagan

I start out with the most important law since it was an epiphany many years ago when I was struggling through mediocrity as a lonely manager. I was adrift and knew it, yet I couldn't overcome my fears and anxiety about leadership.

As I sat exasperated at my desk wondering how I would be a success and make a difference in my organization I realized that throughout my career I had watched and dutifully mirrored those that had exemplified leadership skills. I was just not ready to lead.

In retrospect, that was OK. And for many of you it might ring true. We must all find our authentic self and leadership voice within our own time frame. These two important elements are the key to laying a successful foundation for leadership. The good news is it exists in all of us.

Let me begin. I'll setup the situation – I had been enjoying a meteoric rise through IT within a professional services organization when it happened – I was promoted to Director of all business technology services.

I knew how to do every function, had built most systems and my fingerprints were all over the processes of the organization. Yet when it came time to be the one who had to get my team to do the things which needed to be done, I realized that leadership is getting others to do something you want done because they want to do it. I was unsure and unaware of my abilities.

Make no mistake the ability to lead and talent was there, I just hadn't found those critical key elements. As many young managers thrust into a leadership position do, I looked towards my colleagues and peers. I specifically eyed two senior managers who I was friendly with, one I reported to and the other had been in similar shoes years earlier.

I made appointments with both to discuss the next steps and to see if I could gain some further insight and advice. Over the next week I met with each and found they were appreciative towards me for seeking them out yet each, in their own way, let me know I was on my own and that's just how it was.

Why did they treat me this way? Because leadership is hard work. It requires grit, tenacity, and time. Without a crystal-clear purpose that drives you, is leading worth the endless hours, the hand-wringing over forecasts and budgets, the reports, the grumbling, the travel? Will it be worth the steadfast devotion to spending more of your waking hours at work than anywhere else?

Without purpose, will you be OK spending your life immersed in your leadership duties, virtually every second of your existence for the foreseeable future?

Think about it……

Now let me highlight the challenge my team faced. The IT team compromised seventeen people covering all aspects of the IT spectrum – from applications to help desk to network services.

I distinctly remember my first day – entering with my coffee, just like I did every day, folks treated me differently. I wasn't imagining it nor was I expecting the change in behavior. Yet there it was staring me right in the face. Folks I had easily joked with, we seemed to strain just to say good morning and discuss the day's business at-hand.

Seems the staff had been through the wringer with my predecessor and although they knew me, they too had questions.

Much too often, people become leaders because doing so was merely the next logical step in their careers. They know what they want to get from the position (i.e. a new challenge, more prestige, and better pay) but many have a tenuous grasp on what they hope to give. Sure, they've got a reason to lead but they are vague about their purpose. This is not satisfactory.

Knowing why you want to lead provides energy to draw upon – a reservoir of vitality much deeper than just finding meaning in your work.

For example, you are a Tier 1 Help Desk staff. You may find meaning in the fact that you are helping someone with their simple issue. But that doesn't mean you will find the work fulfilling.

Consider this distinction: Meaning is a matter of context — of understanding how your work adds value to someone, somewhere.

Conversely, purpose is deeply personal. It is about finding your place in the big picture; it is about thoroughly loving what you do; it is about being so energized by your calling you feel compelled to shout at the top of your lungs, "This is what I was meant to do!"

At this point I looked towards a leader that had inspired me since I was kid, Thomas Jefferson. I had visited his home at Monticello and came away impressed by his wisdom and actions.

I saw the essence of a leader who understood the struggle in finding those key elements. Jefferson is famous for many things, yet I continue to refer to this singular quote for guidance; "Do you want to know who you are? Don't ask. Act! Action will delineate and define you."

These words helped me to find my purpose in IT. After much reflection I arrived upon the realization that my greater cause was to take tired, toxic cultures, and devote my efforts to transforming them and turning them around.

In a sentence, my purpose has been: to help leverage technology to build world-class organizations that thrive in the face of adversity. Yet I never would have arrived at this succinct encapsulation, which anchors me to my purpose, without first asking this most crucial question of myself: Why Do You Choose to Lead?

From that moment onward, I was never the same. I had taken the first step in becoming a leader. And my team took notice. They too wished to know why I had become a leader.

By stating my purpose, it let them see my authentic self. There were no hidden agendas, just a leader eager to take his team to the next level. Over the next several weeks we developed goals that put our team and the organization onto a greater path which far exceeded the expectations of senior management.

Everyone from the mailroom to the boardroom was invigorated by our attitude and teamwork. Over time I was asked by many of my colleagues for advice on how to build high-performing teams and I always tell them it starts with the most crucial question which one must answer.

As you find yourself on this journey or leadership quest designed to increase your knowledge and perspectives, seek inspiring leaders of your own choosing to find invaluable wisdom that assures you positive leadership growth and development.

PAGE INTENTIONALLY LEFT BLANK

2 YOUR TEAM CAN ONLY BE GREAT IN AN ENVIRONMENT OF TRUTH, INTEGRITY AND TRANSPARENCY

"You have the right to remain silent, but you can never, repeat, never lie or shade the truth."
— Robert L. Woodrum

Leaders make a difference by empowering their team through truth, integrity and transparency. Good leaders maximize their influence with their teams by sharing the vision, yet these foundational characteristics are essential to becoming and maintaining leadership. Let's look at each closer.

Truth or truthfulness refers to honesty, both personally and professionally. Partial truths are avoided so not to mislead others even though they might be technically accurate.

Integrity is used synonymously with truth however it has a different meaning. The meaning of truth refers to the spoken word while integrity deals with the consistency between words and deeds.

When we refer to data integrity in software, we mean that the data is consistent without corruption.

Finally, transparency refers to building trust and loyalty; transparent leaders engage the passion of their employees and leverage their commitment to deliver on the core values of the team and organization.

What people expect from leaders is usually rooted in the basic interpersonal operation of the leader-follower relationship, where personal connections are made through trust, integrity, and transparency.

Here I was placed by the CEO and the Managing Partner of our company on a critical project that required staff from different departments of the organization. A client of significant value, close to a third of revenue had some serious questions regarding our service and billings. They had demanded reports which entailed data we had never captured.

I was charged with building a system, processes and managing a project of administrative, paralegals and attorneys to review documents, locate and capture critical data elements and produce reports as we went along.

The Managing Partner had negotiated this project which was taking on more of an audit like atmosphere. The client had demanded we generate reports weekly to insure we were progressing at a satisfactory pace.

The result was within eight weeks we had to sort, review and capture data from over 7000 cases, encompassing 350,000 documents. And we had one shot to get it right.

All documents needed had been pulled from and stacked floor to ceiling within one of our conference rooms, which became affectionately named the War Room.

The Managing Partner felt these high-priced timekeepers would work best if they had one of their own overseeing the project. He aptly named an up-and-coming junior partner to lead the team. He was charming, quick with the wit and even quicker with abandoning his duty.

No sooner had we started when he grabbed most attorneys and paralegals to work for him on his cases while leaving me with just the administrative staff. Darkness soon fell on this project since we were coming to the end of the first week.

I had the fortune of arriving early to work that Friday, only to be met on the elevator by the Managing Partner. He immediately asked how the project was going and I felt a sudden coldness and was cringing (on the inside).

I had to make a quick decision on what to say. Here is where understanding these foundational characteristics of leadership – trust, integrity and transparency come into play.

I looked at him square in the eye for a few seconds letting the elevator make its way to our floor. As we exited, I stated that we were not doing as well as expected. The Junior Partner had not been doing his part to keep the project on track. I further let him know that at the rate we were moving I sincerely doubted we'd make the deadlines within the scope he'd negotiated with the client.

There was an awkward silence between us, the kind that you're never too sure how it will go; he could seek to fix blame or find a solution. He chose to find a solution. His demeanor was always one of calmness and he grabbed me by the arm thanking me for my honesty. He motioned to follow him towards the War Room.

As we walked inside, we came across a mess of boxes and documents strewn around. Several administrative staff were working but not hard. The Junior Partner and his crew of paralegals and attorneys were nowhere to be found.

We then walked to his office finding him and several others discussing the upcoming March Madness. The mood changed dramatically, and the noise grew to a murmur as the Managing Partner told everyone to get themselves into the War Room immediately.

As we all arrived at the War Room, he didn't ask for explanations just for answers on how we would get this project kick started and meet our deadlines.

The room grew silent and I was waiting for the Junior Partner to comment yet he never did. I stood up and stated that I had ideas on how we could get this project back on track. Everyone noticed, smiles took hold and a breath of fresh air seemed to move about the room.

And from there we worked together and made a success out of this project. What are the takeaways…

The Impact of Integrity can never be understated. Good leaders are consistent and as a result those that follow can predict what a leader will do.

When the rules of engagement are not known, a team becomes distracted trying to understand this week's rules. Often a team will become consumed with political gamesmanship and seeking to become the new "favorite".

The Ability to Empower is essential. Good leaders with integrity create an environment where a commitment exists to do the right thing.

Those that follow are assured that they will be supported when acting in integrity and making a difficult decision. Others can act without fear of retribution.

The Air of Confidence is critical. A leader's integrity will not be shaken even in the most difficult circumstances or when the toughest decision must be made.

PAGE INTENTIONALLY LEFT BLANK

3 LEADERSHIP BY OSMOSIS DOESN'T WORK

"Leadership is not about titles, positions, or flow charts. It is about one life influencing another."
-John C. Maxwell

For many years I have been interested in, and fascinated by, the subtle effect a leader can have on an organization.

A leader's style seeps deeply into an enterprise affecting people and decisions the leader will never know about, at least not individually, but collectively it is a far different and powerful story—one played out daily in businesses. We all know these types which can best be described as "closed-minded".

A far better descriptor and analysis of leadership osmosis is when the character and temperament of the man in the corner office courses through hundreds of smaller decisions, often which seems like they are thousands of miles away.

Consider, if the leader is supple and open-minded those decisions made many layers below him are more likely to be agile and empirical. If they are stubborn and too sure that he has all the answers, the modeling of his behavior is likely to result in decisions you will roll your eyes for – which describes osmosis at its worst.

Let's explore this more. Like most people, we've all worked somewhere and muttered "We're in the dark here" or "Nobody knows what's going on".

These are classic signs of a failed leadership technique which is common.

It makes you wonder, based upon its continued rate of failure, why is this technique still around? Why do you hear your colleagues muttering the same thoughts?

Briefly, it is reasoned that developing and implementing a real communications strategy that assures knowledge absorption throughout an organization takes a lot of hard work, especially by the leader.

Many are not up to the challenge. It's predicated on the leader getting out from behind the desk, and to communicate. And not just in the hallways of the corporate office.

A consistent message must be sent out, and reinforced, over and over and over again. It is not a leisurely email about "housekeeping issues". It is using every communication means at the leader's disposal – email, corporate intranet, blogs, video and person-to-person.

On good advice, it's been stated that you can't measure and manage the employee experience without testing and retesting Knowledge absorption. If that involves the leader meeting and greeting employees about their knowledge, so be it.

And that is what I've done! I was never a believer of Leadership by Osmosis. Once upon a time I developed a requirement that EVERY employee in my department could recite our service mantra based upon 3 key operating metrics (and the latest measurements), and our company mission statement, if I saw them and ask them.

It was provided to each employee upon hiring, it was displayed on our terminals, it was printed as business cards to keep handy and it was posted above the door to view upon exiting.

The basis of any key operating metrics is to keep it simple. For me it was about 3 important elements that defined us to our organization.
Provide everyone with the tools to succeed.
Always provide world-class customer service.
Make sure the company makes a profit.*

[Profit can have a semantic value based upon the organization being profit or non-profit based. The first being the value of money whiles the latter is fulfilling the mission through meaningful and purposeful activities.]

And oh yes, I asked. I traveled the halls of our organizations, thousands of miles to our regional offices to test our knowledge absorption.

Was worth it? You bet it was because I didn't assume that they knew. I KNEW they knew. The company was much better off, and more successful, and I never heard those classic lines......

The light was on!

All of which begs the question: As a leader, what osmotic effect are you having on your organization?

Don't succumb to the temptation to try Leadership by Osmosis – put in the work. Go that extra mile. Don't assume anything for making sure everyone knows what they're supposed to know.

PAGE INTENTIONALLY LEFT BLANK

4 MY WAY OR THE HIGHWAY ISN'T THE ONLY WAY

"The best executive is the one who has sense enough to pick good men to do what he wants done, and self-restraint to keep from meddling with them while they do it."
- Theodore Roosevelt

I see a lot of folks in leadership roles (don't ask me how or why they got there) that have that "It's my way or the highway" mentality. These are usually the "leaders" that constantly yell out the word "TEAM" yet, they are not flexible.

Some people think their way is the only right way of doing things. You may be one of those people. Tell me, is it worth it?

Wouldn't it be nice if one way did it right? No matter where you are or who it is–there's only one way to direct, encourage and discipline?

Recently, I advised a friend on his sales team. In effort to enhance the productivity of his team, he debriefed me on each personality, their role and what's been happening at the office.

He has an abrupt, impatient approach with others. His leadership style required more diplomacy, open-mindedness and flexibility. So, I advised…

Leaders succeed due to their ability to accept their follower's behaviors and allow them to complete their duties the best way they see fit. You need to be a chameleon, taking or accepting each of your follower's methods so as it meets the vision or goal.

When attempting to change or force followers to adhere to different methodology you'll be in for a long road of suffering on both ends, since they'll never feel comfortable and you'll feel neglected.

Granted sometime challenges and friction can lead to some great breakthroughs and insight. However, you can gain new insight if you were to be more flexible. Some may feel being flexible means they are weak or that they are caving in to the other person or circumstance.

However, that is not true. When you are flexible you are being open. Open enough to do what may be best for you, and everyone else involved.

To be leader of a team, one must allow the other members of the team to do what needs to be done without placing many attachments on how it gets done. They are not being open to new ways of doing the same old thing, nor are they allowing the "TEAM" a chance to show their skills, talents or even to openly contribute. Instead they are hindering the "TEAM" by being unbendable.

Let's look closely and inspect this leadership strategy. It worked back in the centuries when making widgets had a defined process and could only be made a way. However, today we live in a much more fluid world with bright, hyper-educated and hyper-connected people. So, what fuels this type of leadership – insecurity!

In organizations, everyone has an opinion and more often your people have thoughts, ideas and suggestions that can be helpful. Yet when that insecurity kicks in; because their thinking that someone else may have a better way, it snowballs. It's not only the insecurity of a better way, it's also from the insecurity that someone else may have another way.

You may need to adjust your attitude and become more flexible, adapting to a situational leadership style. Just as we periodically measure and adjust our organizational focus to accommodate changing economic, financial and political environments, I believe it's equally important to measure and adjust our leadership styles to stay relevant and effective.

Becoming an empowering leader allows you to set clear limits of authority, establish shared and measurable goals, and be able to restrain empowered employees from running amok. With planning and management, an empowered environment can be very innovative and entrepreneurial. But left unchecked, it can spiral out of control and the inmates can take over the prison.

That's when becoming a servant leader, which might often be found in smaller organizations and not-for-profits, sees you working side by side with others to provide direction. When you lead by example, you demonstrate you're not above doing the work expected of others. This style can garner the respect of others and can be inspirational.

What does it mean to be flexible? You surrender or give up your preconceived notion about people, circumstances and the way things should be done.

Yet, you may think you are winning when you are always struggling for power and control; believe me you are not winning! If you don't see the good in others and what they offer, you will eventually, become torn down and broken in your quest to be powerful and in control.

Maybe what you need is to take a ride on the open highway and as you drive along admiring the lovely scenery, you notice all the turns and bends in the road and enjoy the flexibility of it all. My Way Or The Highway Is Dead.

Leaders, it's paramount that you listen to your people, involve your people, learn from your people and embrace the reality that the collective sum is much better than the single input of the My Way Or The Highway Leader.

And if that's how you roll.... Well you're dying!

PAGE INTENTIONALLY LEFT BLANK

5 LEAD WITH TRANSPARENT FAIRNESS

"Give as few orders as possible,' his father had told him once long ago. Once you've given orders on a subject, you must always give orders on that subject."
- Frank Herbert (from Dune)

Growing up most of my life, I was told to respect and abide by the Golden Rule. You know, treating others in the same way you'd like others to treat you. On the surface, this has always seemed like a noble and well-intended rule.

I expect you have heard of and/or experienced a situation where two people have the same/similar job title and pay, yet one is a high producer and the other is not. This gets much worse when the low producer gets paid more or has more "status." What rankles the high producer and others around the low producer most is when they "get away with it!"

One of the fastest paths to low morale in a team and organization happens when fairness gives way to sameness. Sometimes this problem arises from misguided "kindness" or "loyalty." Often it is motivated by the leader's inability to engage in difficult conversations or deal with conflict.

Left unattended, your best people will get sick of it and either stop performing or leave. The worst performers will drag down the organization. Fairness happens when everyone understands the expectations/rules/norms and holds themselves and each other accountable to them.

The truth is people are different. They have different likes, dislikes, goals, plus motivators. It was from this lesson, I discovered a new Golden Rule…

Treat others with transparent fairness. Looking back, if I had followed this rule, I would have known the high producer was frustrated and addressed the fact they were dissension amongst the ranks. In doing so, they would have received the acknowledgement of fairness in a way that was energizing to them!

The more I thought about this rule, it hit me. It applies to everyone – from the people you work with, to the people you live with. Every time I follow this new paradigm of thinking, I've found the results more positive and rewarding.

I realize this "new" Golden Rule requires extra effort. To follow this way of thinking, you need to really know the other person and how they want to be treated and recognized. You need to know what makes them tick, then call on that knowledge when engaging with them.

Trust builds in that space and distrust builds when no one pays attention, particularly when the no one includes the leader. In over 25 years of leading many people in many roles, I have not had ONE law suit, a grievance, or arbitration because I treated people fairly.

The people who experienced those problems were often leaders who held no one accountable, held people to different standards, or held everyone accountable for the actions of a another(s). Fairness has ALWAYS been one of our most deeply imbedded human barometers. We know fairness when we feel and see it – and we know it when we don't.

When you model and lead with transparent fairness, you will be trusted more. You will be respected and appreciated for your fairness, even from those not performing up to par.

I admit this is not an always easy task. Not everyone is good at it. There is no short-cut here. It requires effort and caring. However, one I believe is well worth it. Plus, it is through application of this "new" Golden Rule that can endear people to your leadership.

My challenge…take the time to get to know those you lead. Understand what motivates them and how they like to be rewarded and recognized. When the opportunity strikes – treat them the way they would like to be treated.

Then... just step back and observe.

PAGE INTENTIONALLY LEFT BLANK

6 HIRE PEOPLE SMARTER THAN YOURSELF THEN GET OUT OF THE WAY

"In a battle between two ideas, the best one doesn't necessarily win. No, the idea that wins is the one with the most fearless heretic behind it."
-Seth Godin

If I gathered most of the successful leaders in a room together and asked what they attribute the success of their business to, invariably, they will say it is hiring the great people they have surrounded themselves with. This is not some self-effacing answer.

Great leaders know that businesses are nothing, but a group of people hired to accomplish a mission. The better the people, the better chance you have of accomplishing the mission. No one climbs to the top of the mountain alone -- it requires a great team and great leadership.

Many of these extraordinary achievers will readily confess that most of their team is smarter, more talented and more skilled than they are.

In fact, they will tell you that is always their objective. I once heard that Jeff Bezos claimed his ardent goal is to always "be the dumbest guy in the room." And candidly, he may not be that smart compared to others at Amazon however he is brilliant at recruiting and retaining great people, people much smarter than he is -- and he owns most of the stock. Sounds darn smart to me!

Why should you hire people who are smarter than you? Wouldn't they be a threat to your job? No. A good leader will surround themselves with the best and the brightest to bring even greater success to a company or project.

Hiring smart individuals is a mark of strong leadership and big-picture thinking. The most popular leadership style, transformational leadership, is based in part on optimally using the intelligence of your followers, rather than supposing you have all the answers yourself.

Surrounding yourself with smart people makes you smarter because it creates an environment that enables you to feed off one another's intelligence, ideas and energy.

True leaders also know how to move out of the way to let others do what they do best. If you're working too many hours and following up on every detail look closer at your team to ensure you've surrounded yourself with the right people.

If you can find people with more passion, more knowledge, and more desire to succeed than you have, it will push you to be better and take the organization to new levels.

Here, I summarize the characteristics I like to look for:

They do things. Smart people know what's required, or can figure it out, and are confident enough to decide without you.

Recommend their ideas. How often do the people around you recommend sound ideas you never knew were possibilities?

Passionate and positive. The smart people you want are as positive and passionate about your business as you are.

More listening than talking. Look for team members who are active listeners, where you can see yourself seeking them out for answers, rather than always the other way around.

Hire for an appetite to learn. Many people say hire from experience. Nothing I've ever done and succeeded at is something I have done before.

Avoid the narcissists. Their energy, self-confidence, and charm make them look smart, but they resist accepting suggestions, thinking it will make them appear weak, and they don't believe that others have anything useful to tell them.

Organizations with the best people win. The job of the leader is to go get the best people you possible can. The key skill you want to build, develop and hone is your recruiting skill. Act like the success of your business depends on it -- because it does.

I've noticed that one of the biggest issues is the lack of executive managerial maturity, where their first concern is their own position and security.

There's a general concern that they want to hire a good, talented person yet if he or she is better than they are, they'd be putting their own position at risk. The issue is not always about smarts.

A manager may be reluctant to hire someone with more education, better experience or better people skills, which may make the candidate, seem better than the manager is. Not wanting to hire someone smarter than you is a common strategy for ambitious people — though a short-sighted one.

Leaders who insist on being the sharpest pencil in the box are afraid to admit that they have any flaws or deficiencies, which often leads to their downfall. This attitude not only inhibits the growth as a leader, it damages the company's bottom line, and stifles their team.

When they can't let go, leaders can be a source of great frustration for employees -- not only because they don't get out of the way, but because they get so wrapped up in day-to-day work, they can't set strategic direction or allow others to excel. This lack of leadership and opportunities for career growth will inevitably cause talented people to jump ship.

Instead, successful leaders should be able to take their eyes off their own goals and focus instead on the good of the organization, which includes upgrading the workforce with team members better at certain tasks.

That thinking requires a brave, creative, and yes, smart leader. When you hire people that are smarter than you are, you prove you are smarter than they are!

PAGE INTENTIONALLY LEFT BLANK

7 IF YOU WANT THEM TO REMEMBER SOMETHING, SAY IT OVER AND OVER (CONSISTENCY)

"A leader takes people where they want to go. A great leader takes people where they don't necessarily want to go, but ought to be."
-Rosalynn Carter

A leader is always on stage and needs to show the same positive and consistent face to his or her audience (the team).

Consistency is a trust builder, it allows for measurement, it creates accountability, while establishing your reputation and makes your message relevant.

As a leader you want to communicate a consistent message for each employee or team. And then you want to relentlessly follow up and focus only on that message.

Your communication [to your team and to your customer] must be clear, consistent and repetitive. You must be consistent in your "brand" message, your "advertising", and your "market presence".

Any common or rapid changes in your message distract everyone and prevent them from forming and strengthening an image of your leadership in their mind. Your consistent performance, message, and presence boost credibility and awareness of your leadership abilities.

It leaves everyone to fully understand what it stands for, and what it can do to help solve the organization's challenges.

While it's easy to understand why a consistent message is important for a product brand, what's often overlooked is how it's equally critical towards leading a team toward a shared goal.

It's only natural that leaders can become reactive to put out the fires around their organization instead of reflecting and reviewing what messages they are sending out because of their actions.

However, it's in these moments that leaders must provide a consistent message and sense of direction to their team to help them feel like they are rising above these challenges that stand before them.

So how can leaders make sure they remain consistent in their message to their team?

Here are three steps that will help you to find your anchor.

Define your leadership value proposition: Leaders must establish a set of values used to not only provide a guide yet to help define how others will view your leadership.

In IT we need to promote collaboration among departments to fuel adoption of technology which assists in our organization's growth.

Now put these values into action: Leaders cannot state these values are to foster collaboration.

Instead, they should help you assess what measures you need to encourage such thinking and approaches within your team.

As collaboration is one of my key leadership values, I define what I will do towards breaking down existing silos which exist in various departments.

Am I inviting other departments to participate in project planning or decision-making processes?

Monitor and review how your team perceives your leadership values. Now with your leadership values defined and being used to affect change, you'll need ideas on what measures you should focus on.

It is an easy trap to think that the message you're sending to your employees is clear and consistent however you must communicate regularly with your team, seeking feedback from them on how they perceive the actions being taken and how it reflects on your leadership.

Taking the time to listen to your team about how they perceive your approach will offer much needed insights into whether your actions are reflecting the leader you want to be for your team.

When something doesn't work as planned, I look back and reflect, asking some serious questions. Did we shift gears too quickly? Did part of the team not deliver on a commitment? Or was the expected outcome off base from the start?

Most of the time, the reason tracks back to lack of consistency - As leaders and professionals, we need to communicate and reinforce our brand and our value proposition every minute of every day. We are after all, constantly under observation.

Consistency may just be the very unsexy and uninspiring element to your leadership style that will help you grow your credibility and allow you to create and sustain a working atmosphere that allows your team members to prosper.

However, send out conflicting messages, acting in a manner dissonant from what people expect, and you will inadvertently start a game of "guess what the boss meant." There are no winners in this game.

Remember, you need to be consistent and easy to read where it counts.

PAGE INTENTIONALLY LEFT BLANK

8 THOSE WHO STUDY FROM THE BEST IN HISTORY ARE DESTINED TO GREATNESS

"People buy into the leader before they buy into the vision."
-John Maxwell

Learn from those who've come before you with some of history's greatest--albeit flawed--leaders.

Leaders have plenty of trouble learning from the lessons of history. Maybe it's because as leaders we're supposed to be like jet fighter pilots, always looking forward and no rearview mirror.

As Warren Buffet once said, "it's more important to look out the windshield than in the rear-view mirror."

However, a few looks in the rear-view mirror of history might help leaders, a few looks back may help prevent the same mistakes that others have committed.

Pearl S. Buck once wrote that "knowledge of history as detailed as possible is essential if we want to comprehend the past and be prepared for the future." History need not repeat itself, but it will if we fail to heed its meaning.

Thomas Jefferson wrote "A nation that expects to be ignorant and free in a state of civilization ... expects what never was and never will be," remarking on his notion on being a veracious reader of history.

The value of learning from past mistakes and successes, these lessons learned, allow us as leaders to make improvements, re-chart and re-calibrate our course.

When we agree and decide that looking over our shoulders at past leadership experiences is more than a good neck exercise, we recognize there is tremendous value in looking in both directions of the road.

So, let's look at what I believe truly matters;

History matters – We're interested not only in avoiding mistakes, but also understanding how important leaders faced monumental challenges and succeeded.

Learning matters – We are always looking for ways to improve performance by absorbing the lessons of the past.

Leadership matters -real leaders will become better leaders.

What better role models to learn from than the towering successes and all too human shortcomings than those who came before us?

They provide a practical guide to leading under similar circumstances.

Survival matters - We engage others to stay informed, learn from history and encourage our employees, friends and family to stay up-to-date and involved.

And what have I learned over the past three decades in leading high-performing teams and from studying leaders from the past...

Here are few of my favorite lessons learned.

Old tricks may work repeatedly, but never overlook new technologies. Overtime they become crucial.

Leaders shouldn't promote those who can follow orders. Empower employees to think for themselves and they'll perform better under pressure, even without orders.

Don't set aside high-potential employees and keep them above the fray.

Leaders must ensure their teams are well trained in all tasks and don't lose their relevance.

Control your temper. Outbursts have limited mileage and, more often than not, make you look foolish.

Yet let the old adage remind us, "There are no mistakes in life, only lessons to be learned.

PAGE INTENTIONALLY LEFT BLANK

9 FACTS ARE STRANGE – IGNORE THEM AND IT WILL BE YOUR DEMISE

"A man who wants to lead the orchestra must turn his back on the crowd."
-Max Lucado

Facts are just that - facts - tidbits of truth. There is no shame in facing facts as they are what they are. Yet although we recognize there is nothing to be gained by ignoring them or denying their existence, we do just the same.

Often, we face challenges and, in our quest, to fix them, insist on wearing rose-colored glasses, which is not how to make great decisions and inspire others to follow.

Selectively choosing the information you need to support the outcome you want, discounting or ignoring facts that oppose your way of thinking about the challenge precipitates a decision-making process you believe will make you popular and into one which isn't necessarily in the best interests of the organization.

Sometimes trying to avoid conflict by saying what others want to hear or at least what the more assertive folks may wish to hear might happen.

Good leaders know that they often will have to decide which are unpopular and will be strongly criticized. They accept it as par for the course and move on.

A good leader acknowledges the facts and exploits them for advantage or eliminates their negative impact. Without this data-driven analysis, leaders would not recognize issues that needed to be addressed.

Facts don't just identify problems; they also point towards solutions and give us compelling arguments to support resulting change.

I've found there are two challenges in dealing with facts. The first is to get the right facts and use them timely and effectively. Many organizations get bogged down in a sea of data that produces little meaningful information.

Others will work to manipulate the data to paint the picture they want, either hiding problems or advancing an agenda. Remember the old adage that "figures don't lie, but liars' figure".

The other challenge is to remember that data is just part of the picture. There are and will always be unquantifiable factors. That is not a justification for ignoring facts however it is a caution not to rely exclusively on them.

For example, leaders often fail to recognize the underlying facts that will transform their organizations. The economy's move from the Industrial Age to the Information Age created new facts that leaders must heed. Just look at newspapers as an example of an industry that ignored facts at its peril.

Always remember that ignoring facts is not a strategy.

PAGE INTENTIONALLY LEFT BLANK

10 LET THEM FAIL

"A good leader leads the people from above them. A great leader leads the people from within them."
-M.D. Arnold

How do leaders balance the need to develop leaders and lead winning teams? The challenge is to create opportunities for others to learn, and that means letting them fail miserably without dire circumstances.

The best leaders know this however and let it happen anyway. So, allow your team to flourish as they work toward the shared vision. Show them the truth about their talents and offer them glimpses of new opportunities.

Let them try new things and learn new skills. And let them fail occasionally as failure is nothing more than learning how to win.

Why let failure happen? Failure is the only way we learn. As leaders we need and want people to learn and grow. Failure is a part of the learning process. If people aren't allowed to fail, they won't learn and without learning, they won't grow.

When we don't let others fail, we strip them of ownership. When we don't let people fail, we decide for them. We don't let them make the final call.

When people don't get to make the call, they don't feel attached to the end result; good or bad. Ownership is important to creating accountability. We want our people to feel ownership for their decisions and the consequences; good or bad.

People must make their own decisions. They must be empowered to decide they think will work best. Preventing people from failing takes away their ability to decide. We must let people chose for themselves.

When people make their own decisions, it creates accountability. We can't hold people accountable for outcomes when they aren't given the latitude to choose for themselves.

When we don't let people fail, it's because we chose for them. We disagreed with an approach, we saw a flaw in the thinking, and we did the work for them. When we step into avoid failure, we are taking over the decision-making process.

Taking over the decision means it's no longer their decision and we can't hold them accountable for the end results. People must be allowed to make their own decision if we want them to experience the consequences — good or bad.

When we let people fail, we are empowering them. We are telling them, "we trust you." People must know they are trusted for their expertise. People must feel valued for what they know and for what they do.

When we don't let failure happen, we strip people of a sense of competence. We send the message that says; I don't trust your judgment and therefore I will do this for you. Do this often and your will create drones, as no one will decide. They will just wait for you.

Let failure happen. Failure is the highway to success. You'll be happy you did!

PAGE INTENTIONALLY LEFT BLANK

11 SUMMARY

Unleash Your Greatest Leadership Potential!

Cutting Edge CIO is about great leadership. It equips you with the knowledge, skills, and passion you need to become the leader you were meant to be. It's a book for any leader who wants to become more effective, strategic, operationally focused, and balanced. It's a book for leaders striving to take control of their destiny and become the best they can be.

It's a breakthrough book, and the time is right. In today's business environment, leaders at all levels are up against intense challenges in a hyper-competitive global arena. You can use these tools to help you calibrate your leadership abilities, so you can focus on your strengths and address weaknesses.

The overall approach of the book is to improve your key tactical competencies (such as communication, critical and strategic thinking, decision making, and talent and team leadership) and integrate them with inner traits like values, character, and beliefs so you can unlock and unleash your greatest leadership potential.

Cutting Edge: CIO illustrates through inspiring stories what research continues to reveal: that when people understand that leadership is a relationship and engage in the practices described above, they are more able to achieve their own personal best and turn followers into leaders.

My goal is to help existing and aspiring leaders. It provides many practical frameworks and models to help you plan and implement the key steps required to become the leader you could be.

PAGE INTENTIONALLY LEFT BLANK

ABOUT THE AUTHOR

Gianna works with technology professionals seeking leadership development, executive coaching/mentoring and career counseling. He is also an information technology expert who has worked with some of the most elite companies in the world to help them achieve their organizational objectives. Gianna often works with business leaders in the areas of executive presence, people development, influencing skills, communication, time management, work/life balance, and developing organizational vision and strategy. In addition to his individual work, Gianna also specializes in helping businesses and organizations develop high performance teams and cultures. With professionals of all levels, Gianna provides the skills to allow them to fully realize their potential. These include concentration, focusing, self-talk, dealing with adversity, visualization, planning/evaluation, performance anxiety and understanding the "zone" of peak performance.

Gianna has a unique combination of training and experience in business, technology and consulting. He received his B.A. in Organizational Leadership. Gianna's business experience includes a prior position as a Director at the NFL. His graduate education includes a master's degree in business administration and is in the process of obtaining a Doctoral degree in Organizational Management. Gianna's significant business background includes previous positions as a COO, Controller, Director and Chief Information Officer. This varied experience allows him to easily establish rapport and credibility with those aspiring to the highest levels of performance in a variety of settings.

Gianna is known for his strategic approach with clients. He realizes performance-based individuals need solutions that deliver results in the real world. He provides his clients with the self-knowledge and practical tools to excel in their professional and personal lives.

I love making new professional acquaintances. Reach out if you want to talk technology, business or basketball. If I can't be of service, I may know others who can meet your needs. After all, creating and fostering relationships, and giving back – is a cornerstone today.

LinkedIn – www.linkedin.com/in/jamiegianna